City **1 2 3**

Zoran **Milich**

Kids Can Press

Counting Collection

1 2 3 4 5 6 7 8 9 10

●

one

1 2 3 4 5 6 7 8 9 10

two

1 2 3 4 5 6 7 8 9 10

● ● ●

three

1 2 3 **4** 5 6 7 8 9 10

● ● ● ●

four

1 2 3 4 5 6 7 8 9 10

● ● ● ● ●

five

1 2 3 4 5 6 7 8 9 10

six

1 2 3 4 5 6 7 8 9 10

● ● ● ● ● ● ●

seven

1 2 3 4 5 6 7 8 9 10

● ● ● ● ● ● ● ●

eight

1234

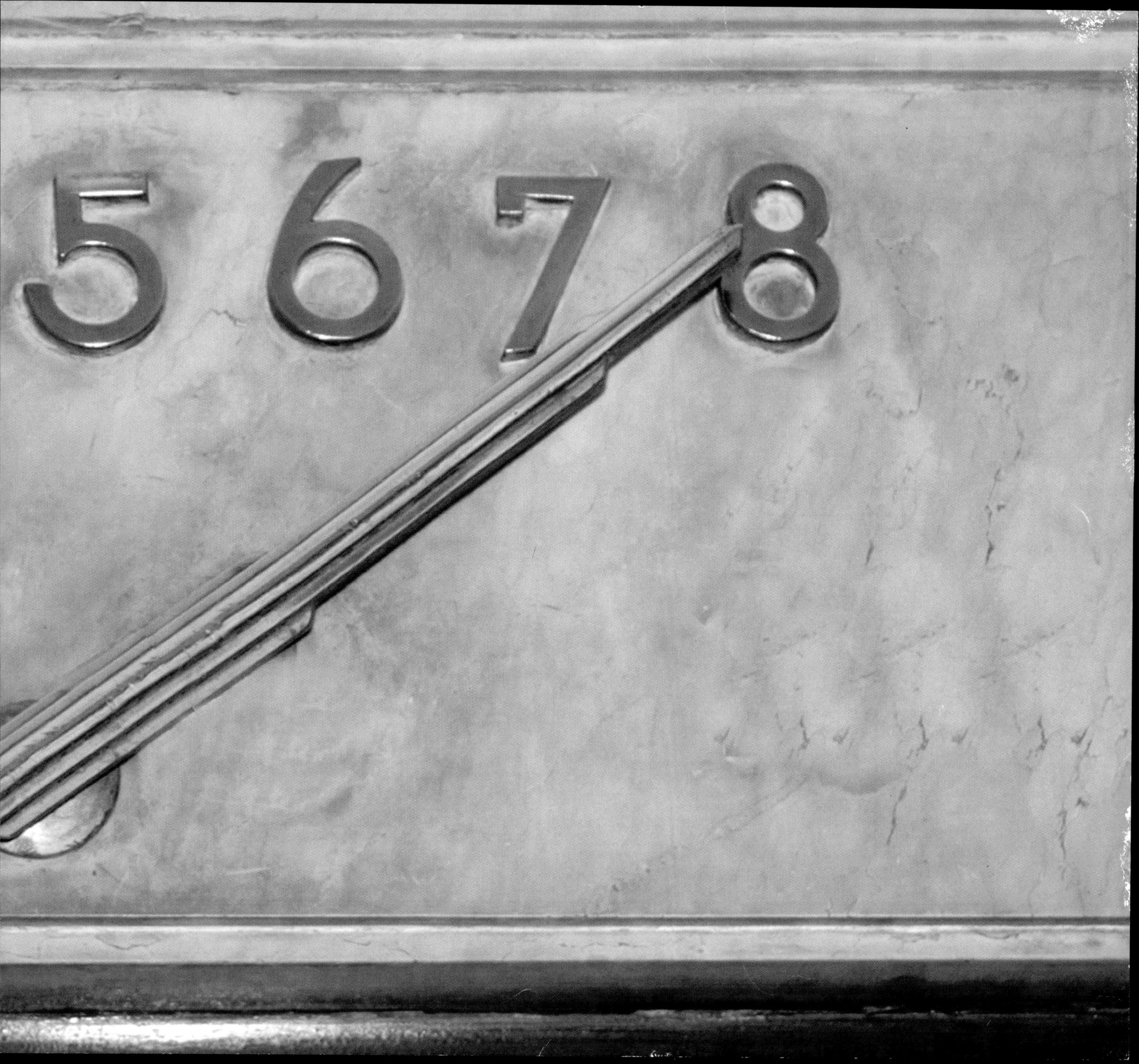
5 6 7 8

1 2 3 4 5 6 7 8 9 10

● ● ● ● ● ● ● ● ●

nine

1 2 3 4 5 6 7 8 9 10

● ● ● ● ● ● ● ● ● ●

ten

Count again.
One to ten!

In memory of the firefighters of Engine 8 Ladder 2, on the scene at the World Trade Center, September 11, 2001.

Kids Can Press acknowledges the financial support of the Government of Ontario, through the Ontario Media Development Corporation's Ontario Book Initiative; the Ontario Arts Council; the Canada Council for the Arts; and the Government of Canada, through the BPIDP, for our publishing activity.

Published in Canada by
Kids Can Press Ltd.
29 Birch Avenue
Toronto, ON M4V 1E2

Published in the U.S. by
Kids Can Press Ltd.
2250 Military Road
Tonawanda, NY 14150

www.kidscanpress.com

Edited by Debbie Rogosin and Sheila Barry
Designed by Karen Powers
Printed and bound in China

This book is smyth sewn casebound.

CM 05 0 9 8 7 6 5 4 3 2 1

National Library of Canada Cataloguing in Publication Data

Milich, Zoran
    City 123 / Zoran Milich.

ISBN 1-55337-540-8

1. Counting — Juvenile literature. I. Title.
II. Title: City one two three.

QA113.M54 2005   j513.2   C2004-901827-2

Kids Can Press is a Corus™ Entertainment company